43

10 —
240

10 —
240

Paul Cézanne

A Painter's Journey

Robert Burleigh

Published in association with the National Gallery of Art, Washington

Harry N. Abrams, Inc., Publishers

Can you become an artist
even if everyone around you
says you can't?

Can you keep painting,
day after day,
if all you hear is "Don't"?

Can you make art that
few people like—and still
believe in yourself?

Paul Cézanne was a serious, determined painter all his life.

Self-Portrait, 1880–1881, oil on canvas, 33.6 x 26 cm (13 1/4 x 10 1/4 in.)

Not easy, is it?

But throughout his life, the painter Paul Cézanne (pronounced *Say-zahn*) answered these questions with a resounding "Yes!" Today, Paul Cézanne is considered one of the finest artists in the history of the world.

Despite the fact that he grew up in a small town where few people cared about art and, as a boy, showed little artistic talent—Paul never gave up. He became an artist and kept painting for more than forty years. He continued to believe in himself (at least on his good days!) all his life. How did he do it? Perhaps a better question is: Why did he do it?

No one knows for sure. We do know that Paul Cézanne was shy, stubborn, self-disciplined, and thoughtful. He was also gifted with a deep love of literature, art, and—perhaps above all—nature.

Much of Cézanne's art combines expressive brushwork with solid forms. *House of Père Lacroix*, 1873, oil on canvas, 61.3 x 50.6 cm (24 1/8 x 20 in.)

Cézanne wanted to transform the beauty and harmony of nature into equally beautiful paintings. He wanted people to see the world as he saw it, to share his vision—to feel what he felt.

"Art is harmony," he once said, "parallel to nature."

Did he achieve his goal? Many people think so. They respect—and love—Cézanne's art. Indeed, the great twentieth-century artist Pablo Picasso called him "the father of us all." If we look briefly at one or two paintings, perhaps we can begin to understand why. Look at *House of Père Lacroix* (1873), painted around the middle of Cézanne's life. It is one of Cézanne's landscapes.

Paul Cézanne with walking stick and backpack,
c. 1874 or c. 1877

Do you see the many greens and yellows in the foreground? Notice how Cézanne painted the leaves on the trees. He did not outline each leaf. Instead, he used many small, rapid brush strokes to build up the thick foliage. The vegetation seems to be growing wildly.

A half-hidden house runs across the center of the painting. Cool shadows play across the orange of the tiled roof. The burst of light on the side of the building makes it stand out from the darker leaves that swirl around much of the painting's edges. The solid form of the house creates a strong contrast to the loosely painted foliage. Do you feel the balance? If you do, you're feeling the power of a Paul Cézanne painting.

Still Life with Peppermint Bottle was painted later than *House of Père Lacroix*. Let's observe it more closely, too.

The apples glow like small lamps, don't they? They vary from yellow to gold to orange to red. But none of them is one simple color. Each is made of many delicately brushed-on shades. The apples seem to hover together, but still remain separate—almost like a small group of people.

The apples are only part of the scene. They are surrounded by the beautiful blues that weave through and nearly encircle the entire painting. The red top and label of the bottle on the left echo the apples' colors, making them even more vivid.

A white cloth seems thrown over the blue drapery underneath it. It appears to be a casual arrangement—but don't be too sure, for Cézanne took extreme care to compose, or place, every bit of the painting! The reflections on the wine-glass and bottles dance before our eyes, along with the hints of white light on the rear wall. These separate parts are all speaking to each other in a kind of play. The color and the composition work perfectly together.

Paintings like these don't just happen, and Cézanne didn't paint just one way. His painting style changed throughout his life to express the ideas that were most important to him at the time.

Paul Cézanne was born in 1839, more than 165 years ago. He grew up in southern France in the small town of Aix-en-Provence (pronounced *ex-on-provonce*). Cézanne's future art was deeply influenced by his childhood world.

Cézanne's father was a successful businessman who had little sympathy for his son's dream of becoming an artist. He wanted his son to pursue what he called "serious" work. All his life, Paul feared and respected his father, but even when they disagreed, his father continued to provide him with a small allowance. Although Paul's father ruled the household, his mother quietly supported the young boy when she could.

OPPOSITE PAGE: The objects in Cézanne's still lifes often seem casually thrown together. But actually they were carefully planned and arranged. *Still Life with Peppermint Bottle*, c. 1894, oil on canvas, 65.9 x 82.1 cm (26 x 32 3/8 in.) THIS PAGE: Aix-en-Provence, Cézanne's birthplace, was a small, provincial French town. *The Market on Peiresc Street in Aix-en-Provence*, c. 1900

Cézanne's boyhood friend Émile Zola (left, c. 1865) became one of France's great novelists. Young Cézanne (right, c. 1861) had a brooding, thoughtful gaze.

At school, Cézanne met Émile Zola, with whom he became good friends. (Zola later became a famous novelist.) When they were boys, Cézanne defended the frail Zola from some playground bullies. Their friendship was important to both of them and lasted for years.

Cézanne, Zola, and a few others often went hiking in the surrounding countryside. They also swam every summer in a nearby river. The beautifully rugged scenery around Aix inspired Cézanne as long as he lived.

Aix was far from the center of the art world. Against the wishes of his father, Paul finally went where every ambitious young French person interested in the arts wanted to go: Paris. In fact, his friend Zola had moved there in 1858, to pursue his writing. Cézanne was twenty-two. For the next several years, he struggled to find his artistic calling.

During this time, Cézanne tried various styles, or ways of painting. He also painted a variety of subjects.

His most ambitious paintings expressed strong emotions. "I am one of the intense ones," he said.

Many paintings he did in the 1860s reveal this intensity. They were shadowy— nearly black (often with bold, contrasting colors). The paint was applied thickly and roughly, and the subjects were dramatic. Listen to some titles: *The Autopsy*, *The Murder*, and *The Abduction*. One observer at the time said the art "looked as if it had been painted with a pistol"!

In the late nineteenth century, Paris was the center of the art world. It was where all the young people who aspired to be painters, sculptors, and writers came to be with other artists. Auguste Renoir, *Pont Neuf, Paris*, 1872, oil on canvas, 75.3 x 93.7 cm (29 5/8 x 36 7/8 in.)

The artist's relationship with his father (right) was a difficult one. His early paintings had a dark, intense feeling.

LEFT: *Antony Valabrègue*, 1866, oil on canvas, 116.3 x 98.4 cm (45 3/4 x 38 3/4 in.) RIGHT: *The Artist's Father*, 1866, oil on canvas, 198.5 x 119.3 cm (78 1/8 x 47 in.)

A portrait, *Antony Valabrègue* (1866) illustrates Cézanne's style at this time. Valabrègue was a poet from Aix and a friend of Cézanne's. The nearly four-foot-high painting shows the subject with a stern and forceful gaze, further emphasized by the clenched fists. The mostly dark clothes, the dark background, and the thickly painted surface all contribute to the kind of intense, barely controlled emotion that marks much of Cézanne's early work.

Even paintings of family members have a similar rough-hewn style. A portrait of his father, *The Artist's Father* (done when Cézanne was twenty-seven), hints at the tension between father and son. Cézanne's father reads a newspaper, sitting near —but not noticing—one of Paul's own still lifes on the wall behind him. Is this perhaps Cézanne's way of saying that his father doesn't care about his art?

This decade of Cézanne's life is sometimes called his romantic period. He worked furiously, often closeting himself in his studio for days. Overall, though, his paintings met with little success. "The sky of the future," he wrote his mother, "looks very dark to me."

As he attempted to develop new painting methods that would take his work further, Cézanne began to take an interest in a small group of experimental painters: the Impressionists. In the 1860s, the Impressionists were artists trying to create a new art style. They felt that much of the art around them was artificial and untrue to nature.

The Impressionists were interested in the effects of light on objects.

They used short, clearly visible brush strokes to capture this effect—or "impression." They also painted outdoors, instead of in their studios, and they usually

worked quickly. Though largely unknown at the time they began painting, today they include many famous names. Three of them—all friends of Cézanne— were Claude Monet, Auguste Renoir, and Camille Pissarro.

In contrast to Cézanne's dark works, the group of artists called the Impressionists used brighter colors. The art movement included artists such as Auguste Renoir, Camille Pissarro, and Claude Monet, and was the most advanced art style in France in the 1860s and after. Auguste Renoir, *A Girl with a Watering Can*, 1876, oil on canvas, 100.3 x 73.2 cm (39 1/2 x 28 3/4 in.)

Paul Cézanne (seated) and Camille Pissarro (standing to the far right) in Pissarro's garden at Pontoise with three young men, c. 1874 or c. 1877. (The youngest is Pissarro's son; the other two are probably artists.)

Pissarro, who was older, took a liking to Cézanne. This was not easy. Cézanne was touchy, easily offended, and sensitive to any criticism. Pissarro invited Cézanne to join him and other artists who were working outside Paris. Cézanne accepted the invitation.

Painting alongside Pissarro, Cézanne's art changed. His colors lightened. His violent subjects disappeared. His brush strokes shortened. He applied paint more thinly. All this is evident in *Landscape near Paris* (c. 1876).

You might say that Cézanne almost became an Impressionist. However, he never really felt that his goals and theirs were the same. So—artistically speaking—he remained an outsider, although he continued to exhibit his work with them.

OPPOSITE PAGE: Under the influence of Camille Pissarro, Cézanne also began to use brighter, lighter colors.

TOP: Camille Pissarro, *Orchard in Bloom, Louveciennes*, 1872, oil on canvas, 45.1 x 54.9 cm (17 3/4 x 21 5/8 in.)

BOTTOM: Paul Cézanne, *Landscape near Paris*, c. 1876, oil on canvas, 50.2 x 60 cm (19 3/4 x 23 7/8 in.)

Here are paintings of the same scene, one by Cézanne and the other by Pissarro. Both men frequently painted the same scene—in this case, an orchard in Pontoise, the village in which they lived. Look at the two works. Are there any differences?

Pissarro's painting is titled *Orchard with Flowering Fruit Trees, Springtime, Pontoise* (1877). It is truly impressionistic. Do you see the quick, small brush strokes that nearly hide the buildings in the background? In his painting of the orchard, Pissarro seems mainly interested in the burst of white light that is reflected off the leaves and fills much of his canvas.

Cézanne's *Orchard in Pontoise* (1877), on the other hand, is far more angular. True, the scene is lighter than his earlier dark paintings, and in places the paint is loosely dabbed on. But the buildings and the low wall remain prominent. Straight edges are visible everywhere. This gives the painting a more structured appearance— a feature of much of Cézanne's work. Because angular forms are more rigid, they often seem less spontaneous and less impressionistic.

OPPOSITE PAGE: Cézanne and Pissarro sometimes painted the same scene. Here Pissarro's more spontaneously applied brushwork contrasts with Cézanne's more structured forms. TOP: Camille Pissarro, *Orchard with Flowering Fruit Trees, Springtime, Pontoise*, 1877, oil on canvas, 65.5 x 71 cm (25 3/4 x 28 in.)

BOTTOM: Paul Cézanne, *Orchard in Pontoise*, 1877, oil on canvas, 50.2 x 60 cm (19 13/16 x 26 5/8 in.)

Cézanne admired many Impressionist painters, but he sought something different in his work. Claude Monet, *Woman with a Parasol—Madame Monet and Her Son*, 1875, oil on canvas, 100 x 81 cm (39 3/8 x 31 7/8 in.)

Cézanne both criticized and praised the Impressionists. "Claude Monet is only an eye," he once proclaimed, "but what an eye!" For Cézanne, capturing the brilliant surface of things was an achievement—but never enough.

Cézanne did show work at Impressionist exhibitions in Paris in the 1870s. The results were disappointing. One outraged critic called him "a sort of idiot who paints in the throes of delirium tremens."

It was time to move on. But where?

In retreat from the disappointments of the Parisian art world, Cézanne decided to return to the place he loved: Aix, and the region of Provence. It was 1880, and he was just over forty years old. He took with him his companion, Hortense, and their young son. Although Cézanne often traveled back to Paris during the remaining years of his life, it was in his native Provence that his art—his still lifes, his portraits, and, above all, his landscapes—truly flourished.

Interior of Paul Cézanne's studio in Lauves, Aix-en-Provence

These four drawings of the artist's young son, also named Paul, all come from one of Cézanne's sketchbooks.

Cézanne's studio contained a variety of simple objects that he used in his paintings again and again.

Objects (a bottle, a tapestry, and pitchers) used by Paul Cézanne as models for his still-life compositions found in the Lauves studio, Aix-en-Provence

Cézanne painted almost two hundred still lifes, focusing on simple household items: a table, a cloth, pots, and fruit—especially apples. Why apples? Did he recall that Zola had years ago given him a basket of apples in gratitude for Cézanne's defending him from bullies? Cézanne loved the rich colors and the basic shape of this common fruit. He also liked the challenge of creating a great painting using homely objects. "I want to astonish Paris with an apple," he once said.

Cézanne set up his still lifes with great care. But when he began to paint, the picture might change in unusual ways. Look at *Kitchen Still Life* (1888–1890). The front edge of the table isn't quite level. The right edge is higher than the left. Most objects on the table are viewed as if from straight ahead. Yet the large pot in the rear is seen from the top! And what about the chair legs at the upper part of the painting? They rest on a floor that is sloping sideways. Cézanne seems to be painting from several different positions, or points of view, at once. Did he make mistakes? No. Cézanne knew what he was doing. He believed that the beauty of the whole painting was more important than anything else—more important even than the correctness of all of its parts.

Cézanne would set up a still life with great care, but when he painted, what he composed on the canvas was sometimes very different. *Kitchen Still Life*, 1888–1890, oil on canvas, 65 x 81 cm (25 1/2 x 31 7/8 in.)

While he worked, he might have asked himself:

Does the painting grip the viewer?
Is the color bold and strong?
Are the parts working together?

If the answer to all these questions was yes, Cézanne was sometimes satisfied. ("Sometimes" because he was very critical of his own work. In fact, he threw away many paintings he felt were not good enough.)

Cézanne's portraits pay equal attention to the face, the body, and the background. It was the "whole painting" that interested him.
Boy in a Red Waistcoat, 1888–1890, oil on canvas, 89.54 x 72.39 cm (35 1/4 x 28 1/2 in.)

Cézanne painted portraits too—most often of himself or of those around him.

In his portraits, Cézanne was as interested in the background as in the person being painted. As always, it was the "whole painting" that mattered most. Observe *Boy in a Red Waistcoat* (1888–1890). The vest, the shirt, and even the background drapery are all painted as expressively as the boy's features. Yet we still feel the thoughtfulness that shines forth from the face. Cézanne painted four versions of this picture, and they are among his most famous works.

Sitting for Cézanne was an exercise in patience. If the sitter shifted his or her weight, Cézanne would shout angrily, "Does an apple move?" One sitter is said to have sat so long that he fell asleep and tumbled over. According to Cézanne, this upset the pose and ruined the picture forever.

Cézanne also painted groups of figures. *The Card Players* (there are five versions) consists of several men playing cards at a table. The models for these paintings were workers on the Cézanne family farm. The paintings, among Cézanne's most popular works, are very compelling. But why the artist chose this subject remains a mystery.

Another series of paintings centers on people bathing outdoors. These paintings show men, or, more often, women, by a river or water's edge. Perhaps Cézanne recalled his boyhood summers swimming with Zola and other friends in the local river.

This is one version of a scene Cézanne painted several times in slightly different ways. *The Card Players*, 1890–1892, oil on canvas, 65.4 x 81.9 cm (25 3/4 x 32 1/4 in.)

Landscapes especially occupied Cézanne during his last decades. Year after year, he explored the region around Aix. It was a countryside, he once observed, that possessed "a sadness that no one has yet sung."

He painted variations of the same scenes again and again: his family home, a deserted quarry, or a red-roofed village seen from afar.

Cézanne never simply copied the entire scene before him. He painted what he called the "motif," that part of the scene he felt was most important.

Most often, he painted a mountain. Mont Sainte-Victoire, about ten miles from Aix, could be seen from his father's house and was not far from a studio Cézanne built in 1902.

Cézanne painted more than sixty versions of what he called "his" mountain. Yet none of the paintings look exactly the same.

In some, the mountain looms up majestically before the viewer, as in *Mont Sainte-Victoire Above the Road of Le Tholonet* (1896–1898). "I think I could be occupied for months," he once said, "without changing my place, simply inclining a little to the right one time and the left another."

OPPOSITE PAGE TOP: *The Road to Le Tholonet and Mont Sainte-Victoire* BOTTOM: *Mont Sainte-Victoire Above the Road of Le Tholonet*, 1896–1898, oil on canvas, 81 x 100 cm (31 7/8 x 39 3/8 in.)

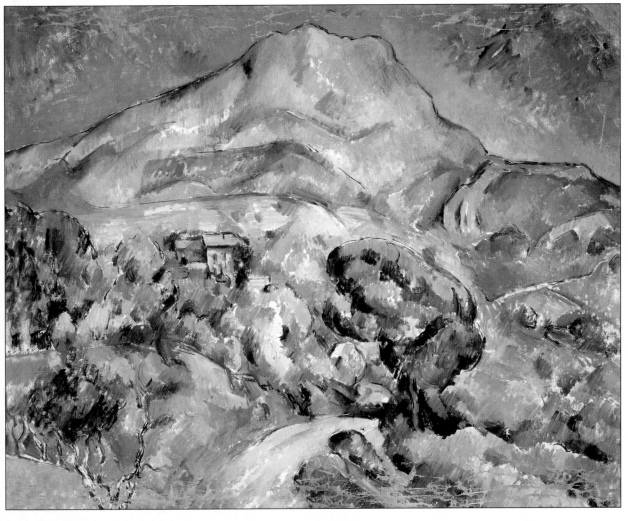

Mont Sainte-Victoire seen from Les Lauves with a tree in the middle ground

No one knows for sure why Cézanne returned to this subject so often. Did he sense in it nature's awesome power? Did it remind him of his own high ambition? Or did it—rising into the sky—suggest to him his isolation from the world?

In fact, Cézanne *was* more alone. In the late 1880s, his father died. Around the same time, his old friend Émile Zola published a novel with a main character loosely based on Cézanne. The character is an artist who despairs of ever painting a masterpiece—and commits suicide. Cézanne was hurt, and he and Zola never spoke to each other again.

His father's death made Cézanne a wealthy man, but his life barely changed. He was a painter—and so he continued to paint. His work schedule changed little.

Mont Sainte-Victoire Seen from Bellevue, 1882–1885, oil on canvas, 65.4 x 81.6 cm (25 3/4 x 32 1/8 in.)

"It's so good and so terrible to attack an empty canvas," he said. Yet attack he did. He arose at dawn and worked in his studio until eleven. After lunch and a brief nap, he was off again—to paint outdoors.

What continued to change, though, was his art. The oil paintings and watercolors of his very last years became simpler and freer.

In his final portraits, such as *The Gardener Vallier* (c. 1905), the subject often seems about to dissolve into the background. Perhaps in this elderly gardener Cézanne saw the image of his own face and body growing older.

As always, Cézanne began his painting with what he saw, such as a man sitting on a chair. But what he saw was powerfully combined with what he felt about the subject.

Cézanne's watercolors (he completed more than 650) were once considered a minor part of his whole career. Today they are thought of as being among his finest work. The drawing is firm. The color is laid down in careful, clear strokes. Many of the watercolors, such as *Still Life with Apples, Bottle and Chairback* (1904–1906) possess a delicate beauty.

In his last mountain paintings, the "realness" of the subject gives way to something more loosely painted. In *Mont Sainte-Victoire Seen from Les Lauves* (1902–1906), the foreground is a series of blocklike greens, yellows, and grays, while the mountain rises in the background like a ghostly apparition. The mountain, it seems, has almost become an object of worship. "I begin to see the promised land," he said.

This is one of the last portraits Cézanne painted.

The Gardener Vallier, c. 1905, oil on canvas, 107.4 x 74.5 cm (42 1/4 x 29 3/8 in.)

In Cézanne's paintings late in his life, the subjects seem almost to dissolve into a mass of colors and forms. LEFT: *Still Life with Apples, Bottle and Chairback*, 1904–1906, graphite and watercolor on paper, 44.5 x 59 cm (19 1/2 x 23 1/4 in.) BELOW: *Mont Sainte-Victoire Seen from Les Lauves*, 1902–1906, oil on canvas, 63.5 x 83 cm (25 x 32 1/2 in.)

Later, many twentieth-century artists would be inspired by Cézanne's work. Pablo Picasso, *Still Life*, 1918, oil on canvas, 97.2 x 130.2 cm (38 1/4 x 51 1/4 in.)

If Cézanne lived as a painter, he also died as one. Painting outside in mid-October 1906, he was caught in a sudden thunderstorm. He lost consciousness. When finally found, he had to be carried home. The artist who had "sworn to myself to die painting," died of pneumonia one week later. He was sixty-seven years old.

His death was an end—and in some ways a beginning. A memorial exhibition was held the following year. More artists, poets, and critics took notice of his achievements.

Largely unrecognized during his life, Cézanne's work was soon seen for what it was: captivating and profound in its own right, and a bridge to some of the twentieth century's boldest art.

Expressionist painters would be inspired by his free use of color. Cubist painters would take further his willingness to portray objects without fixed positions. Abstract artists would be drawn to his simplified forms.

Cézanne stands for those artists who dedicate themselves completely to their art. He was given little encouragement as a young man. He was mocked by critics for many years. Still, he worked on. He was, in truth, a "painter's painter." "I have made some progress," he modestly remarked toward the end of his life.

The proof of this progress lies in Paul Cézanne's work: his paintings, watercolors, and drawings that continue to move us deeply today.

Cézanne painted nearly every day until the end of his life in 1906. *Paul Cézanne finishing his work on the hill of Les Lauves,* 1906

Glossary

(The definitions of the following terms relate to their use in art.)

balance: the way that the main parts have equal "weight" or importance in a work of art

composition: the way that the parts of an artwork are combined or related to make a unified picture

harmony: when all the parts of an artwork combine to form a pleasing whole

motif: for Cézanne, the most important part of a scene that becomes the focus of a work of art

point of view: the position from which something is seen or considered

romantic: art that emphasizes strong feeling and self-expression

series: a group of artworks related in content or style

shade: the slight differences in the same color

still life: an artwork that represents things that are not animated or alive, for instance, fruit in a bowl, chairs, or cut flowers in a vase.

style: the way in which features are combined to express an artistic idea

Select Bibliography

Hoog, Michel. *Cézanne: Father of Twentieth Century Art*. Harry N. Abrams, New York, 1994

Lewis, Mary Tompkins. *Cézanne's Early Imagery*. University of California Press, Berkeley, California, 1989

Murphy, Richard W. and the Editors of Time-Life Books. *The World of Cézanne*. Time-Life Books, New York, 1968

Rewald, John. *Cézanne, a Biography*. Harry N. Abrams, New York, 1986

Schapiro, Meyer. *Paul Cézanne*. Harry N. Abrams, New York, 1988

Verdi, Richard. *Cézanne*. Thames and Hudson, London and New York, 1992

Some of the places you can find the work of Paul Cézanne

United States: National Gallery of Art, Washington; The Museum of Modern Art, New York; Philadelphia Museum of Art; Art Institute of Chicago; Los Angeles County Museum of Art; Cleveland Museum of Art. **Canada:** Montreal Museum of Fine Arts. **United Kingdom:** National Gallery, London. **France:** Musée du Louvre, Paris.

Author's Note

For me, Paul Cézanne is both a difficult and an easy artist to introduce to young readers and viewers. Difficult because he was (and still is) closely identified with many theoretical art issues. Easy because his work is there to see. We do not have to probe the idea of simultaneous points of view to be ensnared by the brilliant colors of a Cézanne still life. Nor do we have to distinguish between Impressionism and Post-Impressionism to be moved by Cézanne's powerful rendition of a weathered house or a shimmering mountain peak.

I have tried to portray Cézanne as an artist who struggled his whole life to capture in paint his vision of the world. To do so, I relied on biographical facts, quotations, anecdotes, and, of course, examples of his work. Although Cézanne was not the most outgoing of men, he did write many letters. A number of other artists, recognizing his importance, left brief biographical portraits and various anecdotes concerning this solitary genius. I have drawn on all these sources. I have also had the aid and assistance of the staff at the National Gallery of Art, Washington, in the selection of which paintings to use and discuss.

I hope readers will understand at the end of the book the hard-won meaning of Cézanne's claim to have "made some progress." Misunderstood by his family, attacked by critics, and living much of his life in semi-isolation, he never stopped working and believing in himself. His life and work hold lessons for everyone. And his art continues to delight us all.

Acknowledgments

I would like to thank those people who helped me in writing this book. At the National Gallery of Art, Philip Conisbee, senior curator of European painting, provided direction from start to finish and Karen Sagstetter, senior editor, and Judy Metro, editor in chief, added many useful points and specific suggestions. My editor at Abrams, Howard Reeves, did likewise, along with guiding the book to its publication. And as usual, a hearty thank-you to my kindest/harshest critic, my wife, Jenny Roberts.

For David Schutter, painter
—*R. B.*

Designed by Celina Carvalho
Production Manager: Jonathan Lopes

Library of Congress Cataloging-in-Publication Data
Burleigh, Robert.
Paul Cézanne: a painter's journey / by Robert Burleigh.
p. cm.
ISBN 0-8109-5784-1
1. Cézanne, Paul, 1839-1906—Juvenile literature. 2. Painters—France—Biography—Juvenile literature. I. Title.

ND553.C33 B87 2006
759.4—dc21

2005011779

Printed and bound in China
10 9 8 7 6 5 4 3 2 1

Harry N. Abrams, Inc.
115 West 18th Street, New York, NY 10011
www.abramsbooks.com
Abrams is a subsidiary of

LA MARTINIÈRE
GROUPE

Illustration credits

Page 1: Paul Cézanne, detail, *Orchard in Pontoise*, 1887, see page 14. Page 3: The National Gallery, London; Image © 2005 The National Gallery, London. Page 4: National Gallery of Art, Chester Dale Collection 1963.10.102; Image © 2005 Board of Trustees, National Gallery of Art, Washington; photo by Richard Carafelli. Page 5: John Rewald Papers, National Gallery of Art, Washington, D.C., Gallery Archives. Page 6: National Gallery of Art, Chester Dale Collection 1963.10.104; Image © 2005 Board of Trustees, National Gallery of Art, Washington; photo by Bob Grove. Page 7: John Rewald Papers, National Gallery of Art, Washington, D.C., Gallery Archives; © Henry Ely; photo by Henry Ely. Page 8 left: John Rewald Papers, National Gallery of Art, Washington, D.C., Gallery Archives. Page 8 right: John Rewald Papers, National Gallery of Art, Washington, D.C., Gallery Archives. Page 9: National Gallery of Art, Ailsa Mellon Bruce Collection 1970.17.58; Image © 2005 Board of Trustees, National Gallery of Art, Washington; photo by Lyle Peterzell. Page 10 left: National Gallery of Art, Collection of Mr. and Mrs. Paul Mellon 1970.35.1; Image © 2005 Board of Trustees, National Gallery of Art, Washington. Page 10 right: National Gallery of Art, Collection of Mr. and Mrs. Paul Mellon 1970.5.1; Image © 2005 Board of Trustees, National Gallery of Art, Washington; photo by Bob Grove. Page 11: National Gallery of Art, Chester Dale Collection 1963.10.206; Image © 2005 Board of Trustees, National Gallery of Art, Washington. Page 12 top: National Gallery of Art, Ailsa Mellon Bruce Collection 1970.17.51; Image © 2005 Board of Trustees, National Gallery of Art, Washington. Page 12 bottom: National Gallery of Art, Chester Dale Collection 1963.10.103; Image © 2005 Board of Trustees, National Gallery of Art, Washington. Page 13: John Rewald Papers, National Gallery of Art, Washington, D.C., Gallery Archives. Page 14 top: Musée d'Orsay, Paris, France; © Réunion des Musées Nationaux/Art Resource, NY; photo by Pascale Néri. Page 14 bottom: Mr. and Mrs. Jay Pack, Dallas, TX. Page 16: National Gallery of Art, Collection of Mr. and Mrs. Paul Mellon 1983.1.29; Image © 2005 Board of Trustees, National Gallery of Art, Washington. Page 17 top: John Rewald Papers, National Gallery of Art, Washington, D.C., National Gallery of Art Library, Department of Image Collections. Page 17 center left: *Head of Artist's Son*, 1888/1889; 1992.51.9.gg. Page 17 center: *The Artist's Son*, c. 1887; 1992.51.9.bb. Page 17 center right: *The Artist's Son Leaning on his Elbow*, c. 1887; 1992.51.9.c. Page 17 bottom: *The Artist's Son Writing*, c. 1887; 1992.51.9.aa. Page 17 sketches courtesy of the National Gallery of Art, Collection of Mr. and Mrs. Paul Mellon, in Honor of the 50th Anniversary of the National Gallery of Art; Image © 2005 Board of Trustees, National Gallery of Art, Washington; photo by Ricardo Blanc. Page 18: John Rewald Papers, National Gallery of Art, Washington, D.C., National Gallery of Art Library, Department of Image Collections; photo by John Rewald. Page 19: Musée d'Orsay, Paris, France; © Réunion des Musées Nationaux/Art Resource, NY; photo by Herve Lewandowski. Page 20: National Gallery of Art, Collection of Mr. and Mrs. Paul Mellon, in Honor of the 50th Anniversary of the National Gallery of Art 1995.47.5; Image © 2005 Board of Trustees, National Gallery of Art, Washington; photo by Bob Grove. Page 21: The Metropolitan Museum of Art, Bequest of Stephen C. Clark, 1960 (61.101.1); Photograph © 1979 The Metropolitan Museum of Art. Page 23 top: John Rewald Papers, National Gallery of Art, Washington, D.C., Gallery Archives; © Henry Ely; photo by Henry Ely. Page 23 bottom: Hermitage, St. Petersburg, Russia; © Scala/Art Resource, NY. Page 24: John Rewald Papers, National Gallery of Art, Washington, D.C., National Gallery of Art Library, Department of Image Collections; photo by Rewald-Marschutz. Page 25: The Metropolitan Museum of Art, H.O. Havemeyer Collection, Bequest of Mrs. H. O. Havemeyer, 1929 (29.100.64); Photograph © 2004 The Metropolitan Museum of Art. Page 26: National Gallery of Art, Gift of Eugene and Agnes E. Meyer 1959.2.1; Image © 2005 Board of Trustees, National Gallery of Art, Washington. Page 27 top: The Samuel Courtauld Trust, Courtauld Institute of Art Gallery, London. Page 27 bottom: Kunsthaus Zürich; © 2005 Kunsthaus Zürich. All rights reserved. Page 28: National Gallery of Art, Chester Dale Collection 1963.10.195; Image © 2005 Board of Trustees, National Gallery of Art, Washington; photo by Richard Carafelli. Page 29: John Rewald Papers, National Gallery of Art, Washington, D.C., Gallery Archives; photo by Ker-Xavier Roussel. Front cover top left: Paul Cézanne, Detail, *Orchard in Pontoise*, 1877, see page 14. Top right: Paul Cézanne, Detail, *Kitchen Still Life*, 1888-1890, see page 19. Bottom right: Detail, *Paul Cézanne with walking stick and backpack*, c. 1874 or c. 1877, see page 5. Bottom left: Paul Cézanne, Detail, *Mont Sainte-Victoire Above the Road of Le Tholonet*, 1896-1898, see page 23. Spine: Paul Cézanne, Detail, *Self-Portrait*, 1880-1881, see page 3. Back cover top left: Paul Cézanne, Detail, *Self-Portrait*, 1880-1881, see page 3. Top right: Paul Cézanne, Detail, *Still Life with Peppermint Bottle*, c. 1894, see page 6. Middle: Paul Cézanne, Detail, *Landscape near Paris*, c. 1876, see page 12. Bottom right: Detail, *Paul Cézanne finishing his work on the hill of Les Lauves*, 1906, see page 29. Bottom left: Paul Cézanne, Detail, *The Artist's Father*, 1866, see page 10.